The World
of Fishes

This book has been reviewed
for accuracy by
David Skryja
Associate Professor of Biology
University of Wisconsin Center—Waukesha.

Library of Congress Cataloging in Publication Data

Takeuchi, Hiroshi.
   The world of fishes.

   (Nature close-ups)
   Translation of: Sakana no kurashikata / text and
photographs by Hiroshi Takeuchi.
   Summary: Discusses the behavior patterns of unusual
ocean fish found in the deep sea or near coral reefs.
   1. Marine fishes—Juvenile literature. 2. Fishes—
Juvenile literature. [1. Fishes] I. Title. II. Series.
   Q L617.2.T3513   1986   597   85-28212

ISBN 0-8172-2548-X (lib. bdg.)
ISBN 0-8172-2573-0 (softcover)

This edition first published in 1986 by Raintree Publishers Inc.

The World of Fishes

Raintree Publishers
Milwaukee

◄ A scuba diver.

With the aid of an underwater camera, this scuba diver is able to take fascinating photos of underwater life. Here a school of fish swims near a coral reef.

▶ Four-striped snappers swimming in a group.

Many fish, including most species of snappers, swim together in groups, or schools. As their name implies, snappers have quick, snapping mouths. They live near coral reefs.

An enormous amount of the earth—about seventy percent of it—is covered with water. That includes freshwater from lakes and rivers and saltwater from the seas and oceans. For centuries, the dark, mysterious underwater world remained largely unknown to man. Then, in the 1940s, with the development of good diving equipment, people began to explore the world of fishes for the first time. Using modern photographic and video technology, scientists have now identified more than 32,000 kinds, or species, of fishes throughout the world. Two-thirds of them live in the seas and oceans.

◀Flat horse mackerals attacking a school of sardines.

Ocean bonitos and various species of mackerals often attack, or prey upon, smaller fish. But if small fish swim in schools, they are less likely to be attacked.

▶ A sea swallow attacking sardines.

Birds like this sea swallow dive from the sky to catch small fish, or sardines, which swim close to the water's surface. The fish on the left is a fleeing flat horse mackeral.

Fish are constantly in danger of being eaten—by birds, people, or other fish. To protect themselves, many kinds of fish travel together in large groups, or schools. Often they swim in perfect unison with one another, as if they were a regiment of finely trained marching soldiers. Herrings, especially, swim in large groups. As many as three billion have been sighted in one school.

▼ A whale shark. The whale shark is the largest living fish in the world. One that was caught off the Florida coast in the early 1900s weighed about forty thousand pounds.

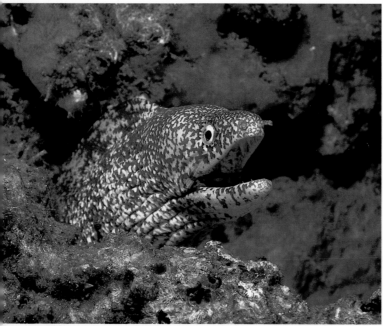

When an octopus is attacked by a moray, it fights back, wrapping its long arms around the moray. Even if it loses an arm or two in the fight, it will not necessarily die.

A delicately balanced food chain provides nutrition for every inhabitant in the ocean. Some small fish eat plankton, tiny plant and animal particles that float in the ocean. Others eat plant life, snails, worms, shellfish, and other sea creatures. Larger fish eat smaller fish. They, in turn, are hunted, or preyed upon, by sharks and killer whales. And the largest animal in the world, the blue whale, feasts on tons of tiny ocean plankton.

The moray's favorite food is octopus. Morays are ferocious looking eels with sharp teeth. They live among coral reefs in warm tropical waters where they lie in wait for their prey.

Although morays are fish, they look more like snakes. Their slender bodies grow as long as five to ten feet. Instead of scales, which most fish have, morays have a smooth, slimy skin, which is often brightly colored.

◄ **A moray (left) and an octopus (right).**

▶ **A fight between morays.**

From time to time, morays fight each other over food or territory. But they do not often fight seriously.

▲ Red lizardfish hiding in the sand.

There are about three dozen kinds of lizardfish in the world. They live in warm, shallow areas of the ocean.

▲ A red lizardfish attacking a cardinalfish.

Cardinalfish are small, usually from two to four inches long. They live near coral reefs.

A number of fish burrow in the mud at the bottom of the sea. Minnows often dive into the ocean bottom when they are threatened by enemies. Crabs hide in the sand to protect themselves. And stingrays burrow in the sand in shallow water to search for clams and other food.

Sand-colored lizardfish easily hide, or camouflage, themselves on the ocean's bottom. They burrow there and wait for small fish, shrimp, or other prey to swim by. Because they have large mouths, they can often swallow their victims whole. Lizardfish are named after lizards because their heads look like the head of a lizard.

Another creature that lives at the bottom of the sea is the sea anemone. The anemone waves its brightly colored tentacles in order to attract small fish. It stings its victims and then gradually swallows them.

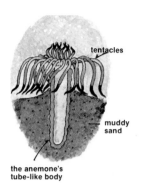

◀ **A purple anemone attracting a small fish.**

The sea anemone becomes active at night as it extends its tentacles in an attempt to attract small fish. But this type of sea anemone most often feeds on plankton. The anemone's mouth is located in the middle of its tentacles.

tentacles

muddy sand

the anemone's tube-like body

▼ **A purple anemone which has just caught a small fish.**

◀ **A trumpetfish waiting for prey.**

This trumpetfish hides its long body behind a branch of coral as it waits for prey to swim near. Trumpetfish average about two feet in length.

Fish often hide among coral reefs and underwater rocks either to wait for prey or to seek protection from enemies, or predators. The trumpetfish is usually found in warm tropical waters near coral reefs. It is brown or yellowish-brown in color and has a long snout for picking up tiny particles of food. The fierce looking scorpionfish prefers to hide in rocky areas in deep water close to shore, as it waits for its prey.

◀ **A long-nose hawkfish hiding among the coral.**

This species of hawkfish spends its entire life hidden among coral reefs. Its color and pattern blend remarkably with the red coral.

▶ **A scorpionfish hiding behind a rock.**

This scorpionfish is almost perfectly camouflaged as it hides among the rocks, waiting for prey. It has poisonous spines which can cause great pain in its victims.

▶ Some fish hide behind other fish.

Here a kaiwari swims behind a pudding-wife. The kaiwari is feared by many fish. So in order to get near other fish, the kaiwari swims along, hidden behind a puddingwife.

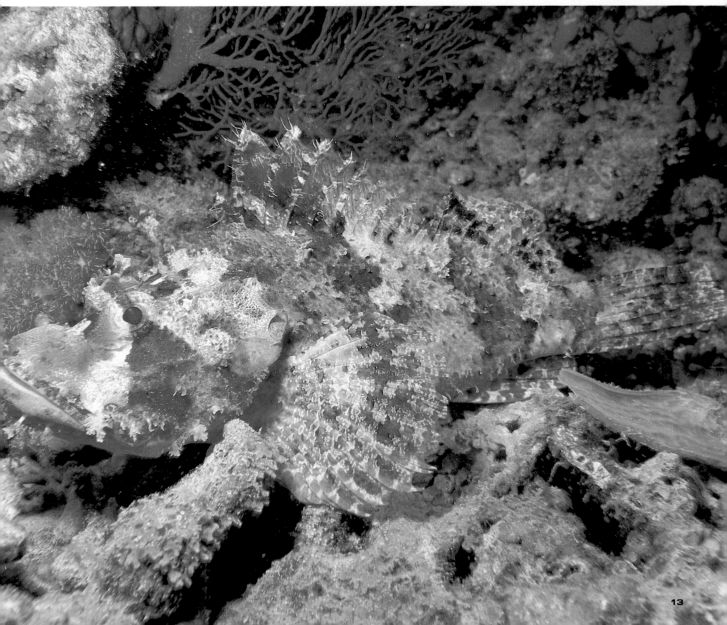

◀ **An ira digs up sand with its mouth as it looks for prey.**

An ira takes four or five mouthfuls of sand from the same place as it digs for food. Smaller fish gather around in case there are any leftovers to eat.

▶ **A goatfish (right) and a seawife (left).**

The goatfish in this photo shares its prey with the seawife next to it. The goatfish is easy to recognize because of the long barbels sticking out from its lower jaw.

Some fish, like stingrays and goatfish, search for food at the very bottom of the ocean. Stingrays live in warm, shallow waters. They lie almost completely buried in the sand. There they feed on worms, lobsters, shrimps, snails, clams, and oysters.

Goatfish live in tropical seas, usually near coral reefs. They have long barbels, or whiskers, which extend from their chins. The goatfish stretches out its barbels over the ocean bottom to look for food. Then it uses its mouth to dig down into the ocean sand where shrimps and crabs are hiding.

◀ **A porcupinefish.**

When it does not feel threatened, the porcupinefish has a square, box-like appearance. Its spines lie close to its body, like hairs.

▶ **A porcupinefish with its spines raised.**

With its body inflated and its spines out, the porcupinefish looks like a chestnut burr. Most predators will not bother such a fierce looking creature.

Fish that can swim fast can easily flee from enemies. But not all fish are good swimmers. Those that are not have other ways to protect themselves from enemies. Members of the swellfish family can inflate their bodies with water or air or both. This sudden swelling of the body frightens off enemies. Porcupinefish belong to the swellfish family. They are found in the warm ocean waters of the world. When porcupinefish are in danger, they quickly gulp water to inflate themselves. As they do so, spines on their bodies stand up, much as the spines do on a porcupine's body when it feels threatened. When the porcupinefish is out of danger, it lets the water out of its body, little by little.

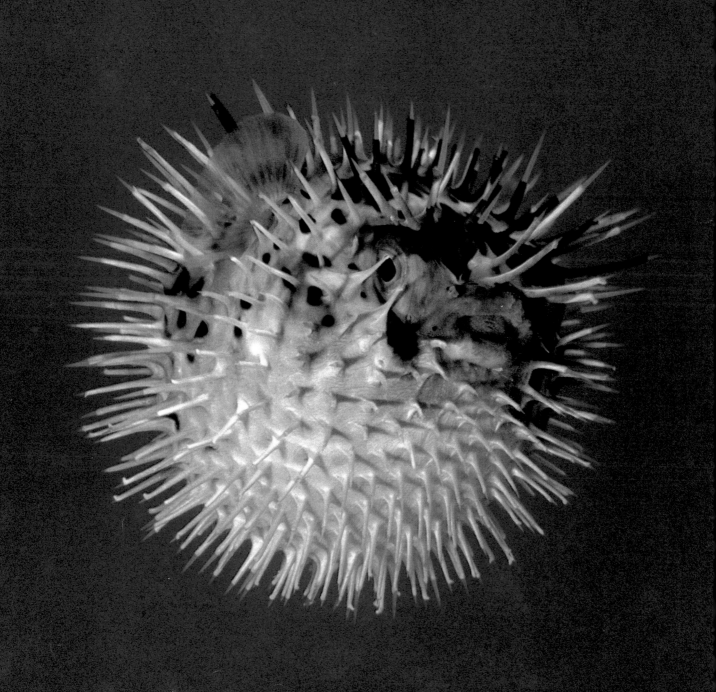

▲ A gurnard spreading its fins to startle an enemy.

As their name implies, most species of sea robins are bright and colorful. They live in deep water in tropical or subtropical seas.

▲ A cicada gurnard spreading its large fins.

Because of their huge pectoral fins, cicada gurnards look several times larger than they really are, and so enemies are frightened off.

Fish swim by contracting their body muscles and using their fins to help themselves gain speed, steer, and stop. But some unusual fish can walk on their fins, as well. Gurnards, also known as sea robins, have specially adapted pectoral fins. The lower part of each fin has three enlarged and separated rays, which the gurnard uses for walking, turning over small stones, and feeling about for food.

Sea robins keep the upper part of their pectoral fins folded up when they are walking. But if the gurnard is startled, it spreads its fins out like brightly colored fans and swims off. Scientists believe the bright colors help to scare away predators. The gurnard also sometimes frightens its enemies by vibrating the muscles of its air bladder, making a loud noise.

▶ The false eye on a hachi fish's dorsal fin.

Scientists believe the black circle on the hachi fish's dorsal fin, which resembles an eye, helps to keep predators from attacking the fish's head and real eyes.

▼ A lionfish with poisonous dorsal fins.

Lionfish belong to the scorpionfish family. Their dorsal fins are very poisonous. Once another fish is stung by a lionfish, that fish will not attack again. The lionfish's gaudy colors also help to frighten off predators.

● **The flounder can change its color.**

Many kinds of flounders can change their colors to blend in with their background. These four photos, taken during the course of three minutes, show how quickly the flounder can adjust its color to changing backgrounds.

A fish's vision seems to vary from species to species. But most fish have two eyes, one on either side of the head. When a baby flounder is born, it looks just like other fish. But within a few days, a strange thing begins to happen. The baby flounder, which had been swimming upright, begins to tilt to one side. As it continues to lean over, the eye on the underside begins to rove upward. Within a few days, the flounder's body has flattened out and both eyes are now located on the top side of its body. The baby flounder's skull and mouth also have twisted around to the top side. The flounder swims or lies at the bottom of the ocean with its blind side down and its two eyes staring up. Sometimes it is the right eye that moves, sometimes it is the left, depending on the species of flounder.

Fish among coral reefs.

A variety of sea life thrives around coral reefs. These reefs are found in warm, shallow water where oxygen and sunlight are plentiful. It may be that the fish have bright colors so that members of the same species can find one another against the brilliant coral background. The fish in photos 1-6 are: (1) A Moorish idol, (2) A black-backed butterflyfish, (3) A two-colored cherubfish, (4) A kind of sea bream, (5) A threadfin butterflyfish, (6) A clown triggerfish.

Brightly colored, intricately patterned coral reefs are found in warm tropical waters. They provide protection for a multitude of fish. The reefs are made up of millions of limestone deposits laid down by tiny sea creatures.

Fish that live near coral reefs are often exotic looking, with brilliant colors and unusual shapes. Bright green, yellow, blue, or orange fish are commonly found in tropical waters. The colors of a particular species may vary, depending on the age and sex of the fish. Some kinds of reef fish have the remarkable ability to change colors altogether— to blend in with a particular color of coral, or with daylight and darkness. Many of them are flat or thin so they can easily swim among the coral reefs.

◄ A hawkfish hiding behind coral.

The hawkfish is a rare kind of coral fish. There are only a few species in the world. They live only in the Pacific and Indian oceans where they spend most of their time resting among coral reefs or defending their territory.

▶ Clown anemonefish swimming among sea anemones.

Most parent fish do not look after their eggs once they have been laid. But clown anemonefish care for their eggs until they have hatched. Sometimes the infant fish stay in the same territory as the adults.

Damselfish are common coral reef fish. Among the best-known members of the damselfish family are the anemonefish. There are about a dozen kinds throughout the world. They are called anemonefish because they can swim in and out of the tentacles of sea anemones without being stung. If an enemy comes near, the anemonefish swims into the waving tentacles of the anemone, out of harm's way. In turn, some kinds of anemonefish help the sea anemone by cleaning its tentacles. Clown anemonefish are the most common of the anemonefish. They are bright orange in color with broad bands of white. They have rounded fins edged in black.

▶ Other types of anemonefish.

The fish in the left photo is the most aggressive of the anemonefish. It will even try to scare off a diver, if one comes near.

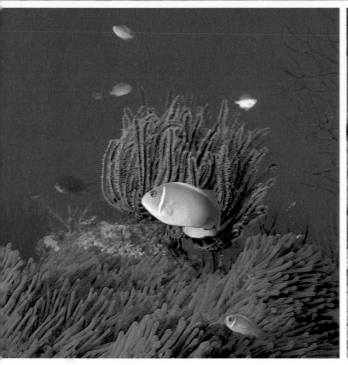

▶ **A cleaner wrasse cleaning a grouper.**

This large grouper stays still as the cleaner wrasse eats parasitic worms from its body. Sometimes a cleaning center is so busy that fish have to wait for their turn to come.

Sometimes fish that would ordinarily be enemies help each other. Certain fish and other sea creatures establish "cleaning areas" on rocky reefs in the ocean. Other fish come by to have their bodies cleaned. The cleaner fish nibble unhealthy tissue and eat parasitic worms from the visiting fish's body. Often, they even clean inside the mouths of their visitors. While the visiting fish has its body cleaned, the cleaner fish gets a free meal and is protected from enemies.

Shrimps and goby fish also help each other. Shrimps dig holes in the sand of the ocean floor to make homes for themselves. They share their homes with gobies, who, in turn, keep watch at the entrance of the hole. If an enemy comes near, the goby warns the shrimp, which cannot see very well.

● **A shrimp shares its home with gobies and sleepers.**

The small, striped goby keeps watch as the shrimp digs a hole in the sand (upper photos). The bright greenish blue and purple fish, a sleeper (lower photo), is closely related to the goby.

▶ Swellfish laying their eggs.

(1) Females that have just laid their eggs. (2) Male swellfish on the beach. (3) The white bubbles contain sperm discharged by the males.

◀ A beach where swellfish lay their eggs every summer.

This species of swellfish comes out of the ocean in early summer to lay its eggs on the beach. Every year the fish come back to the same place. About two hours before high tide, many females gather on the beach where they lay their eggs. Then the males come up on land to discharge sperm. The sperm join with the eggs and fertilize them. Later, the tide carries both the adult swellfish and the eggs out to sea.

▶ A swellfish swimming near the bottom of the sea.

Swellfish are suitably named because they can make their bodies swell up by gulping air or water. Some species are good to eat, but others are poisonous. Swellfish are considered a delicacy in Japan.

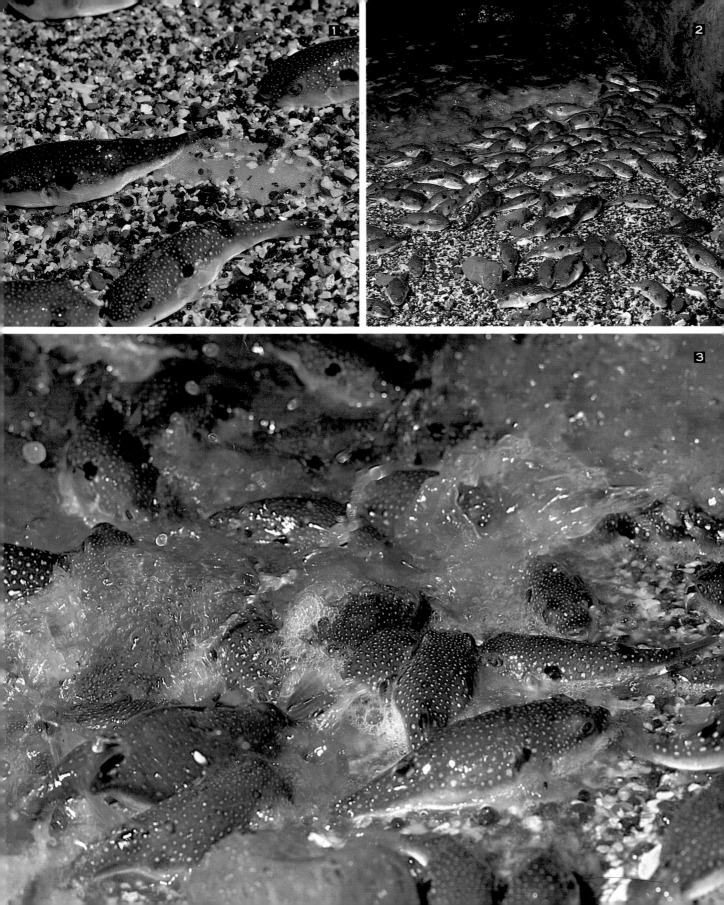

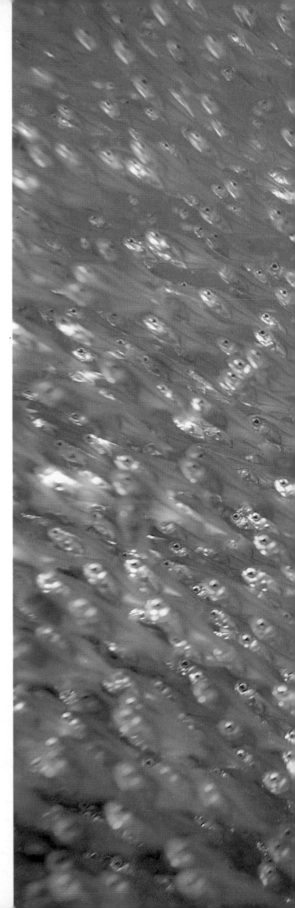

▶ **A group of young porgies.**

Porgies typically travel together in large schools. Many species of fish lay thousands of eggs because life in the ocean is hazardous. Only a few of the many fish in a school like this will survive to reach adulthood.

The eggs return to the sea on the tide and soon hatch. There is plenty of food in the ocean for the infant swellfish. They eat and grow quickly. But only a few of them will survive to become adults because many other fish prey upon the young swellfish. And, in turn, still other fish prey upon the predators of the swellfish. And so it continues, with each inhabitant playing a part in balancing the intricate life cycle of the sea.

▼ The ocean at sunrise.

GLOSSARY

barbels—the long whiskers on the goatfish's chin, which are used for probing the ocean bottom for food. (p. 15)

camouflage—to hide by blending with the environment. (pp. 9, 12)

dorsal fins—the fins on a fish's back. (p. 19)

fertilize—when a sperm and an egg unite, making it possible for a new organism to form. (p. 28)

parasitic insects—those which live off other animals, often causing injury or death to the host. (p. 27)

pectoral fins—a fish's front fins. (p. 18)

plankton—tiny particles of plant and animal life that float in the water. (pp. 8, 10)

predators—animals that hunt and kill other animals for food. (pp. 12, 16, 18)

prey—animals that are hunted by other animals for food. (pp. 7, 8, 9)

school—a large number of fish of one kind swimming together. (pp. 4, 7)

species—a group of animals which scientists have identified as having common traits. (pp. 4, 7, 18)

sperm—a mature male germ cell. (p. 28)